TODAY'S TECHNOLOGY

Written by Alan Aburrow-Newman

TOP THAT! Kids™

Copyright © 2004 Top That! Publishing plc,
Top That! Publishing, 27023 McBean Parkway, #408 Valencia, CA 91355
Top That! is a Registered Trademark of Top That! Publishing plc
All rights reserved
www.topthatpublishing.com

Contents

Introduction	3
Cars and Bikes	4
Planes	8
Boats	12
Submarines	14
Computers	16
Computers and the Internet	18
Computers and the Home	20
Robots	22
Satellites in Space	26
Telecommunication	28
Technology and the Environment	30
Gadgets and Gizmos	32
Lethal Weapons	36
Rockets	40
Space Exploration	42
Spectacular Failures	44
Glossary	46
Finding Out More	48

Introduction

It's amazing to think that things we take for granted today, from computers to telephones, didn't even exist 200 years ago.

Facts and Stats

In *Today's Technology*, you'll find out all about the astonishing technology humans have at their command today—from machines that can travel faster than sound and can take astronauts into space, to those that allow us to keep in touch with people on the other side of the world.

World Wonders

From the earliest inventions to the hi-tech wonders of the world around us today, you'll be amazed at how technology has progressed over the past centuries. Do you know how we got from the world's first self-propelled vehicle to a car capable of breaking the sound barrier? Or that there is a ship called *The World* with nearly 200 fully furnished homes on board?

Where Next?

This book will help you see how far mankind has come in just a few centuries. But how much further can we go? What new technological boundaries can we break? Perhaps it is only a matter of time until we are able to visit a museum about the Internet!

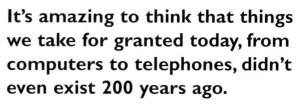

Cars and Bikes

The last 200 years or so have seen the most significant developments in transport since the wheel was invented around 3000 BC.

The first car was made by Karl Benz.

First Self-propelled Vehicle

In 1769, French military engineer Nicolas Cugnot mounted a steam engine on the back of a huge timber-built truck and created the world's first self-propelled vehicle. Two years later, Cugnot was also responsible for the world's first recorded motor accident, when he lost control of one of his motor cars and demolished a Parisian wall. He notched up a hat-trick of firsts when, after a string of crashes, he became the first motorist to be jailed for dangerous driving!

Four-stroke Gas Engine

Since Cugnot, motor car designers across the world have competed to build ever-faster and more sophisticated machines.

Nicolas Otto invented the four-stroke gas engine in 1876. At that time Otto's engine was capable of propelling a car at about 5 mph (8 km/h). Today's supercars achieve speeds of over 186 mph (300 km/h)!

Benz, Levassor and Panhard

Karl Benz bolted one of Otto's engines onto a

Cars and Bikes

Ransome Eli Olds was the first to mass-produce cars.

trike and called it a car. Emile Levassor and René Panhard placed the engine in the front of their car, added a changeable gearbox, and gave the motoring world the true forerunner of modern cars. Between them, they certainly managed to start something!

Assembly Line
Ransome Eli Olds was the first person to mass-produce cars to be sold in America. He introduced the assembly line system and set up a factory in Detroit. Sadly, the factory burnt down before production could begin but Olds did produce "The Oldsmobile Gas Buggy." This little car was highly successful and sold in large numbers many years before Ford started building cars.

Ford
Henry Ford's "Tin Lizzie" was once the world's best-selling car, having sold over fifteen million units. However, the Volkswagen Beetle has now sold over 40 million since it was launched in 1936.

The Thrust SSC.

Alternative Fuels
Finding alternative energy technology for cars has been a major challenge. The only working options are solar power, electrical, or alternative fuels such as hydrogen.

In July 2000, a solar-powered car took 29 days to complete an astonishing 4,377 mile (7,043 km) journey across Canada from Halifax to Vancouver. The "Radiance Solar Car" runs on as much energy as a toaster!

Speed
The *Thrust SSC,* driven by Andy Green (UK), was the first land-based vehicle to break the sound barrier. On 15 October 1997, it achieved a two-run average of 763.035 mph (1,227.985 km/h)!

Cars and Bikes

Fastest Production Cars

The development of supercars for the road has taken a great deal of technology from Formula One racing, and some of the most expensive and sought-after dream cars have evolved from this fast-paced sport.

The "McLaren F1" is the fastest production car on the road to date. With an awesome 550 horsepower V12 engine and a body of space-age carbon fibers, it is capable of speeds in excess of 278 mph (448km/h). McLaren only made 100 F1's before taking the car out of production. However, McLaren will struggle to hold onto their crown, as other car companies race to create an even faster monster.

Bugatti looks likely to be the winner with their astonishingly powerful "Bugatti Veyron." The Veyron has no less than 1,000 horsepower at its disposal, and threatens to obliterate the McLaren F1's awesome performance records.

Bikes

The first motorcycle was invented by accident in 1886 by Gottlieb Daimler. He was actually developing a car engine and fitted it into a two-wheeled contraption to test it. Daimler's cycle had stabilizer wheels so was technically a four-wheeler.

Development

As motor engines were being developed, it was hard enough for builders to get their machines to work without worrying about them falling over so the development of

The "McLaren F1," the fastest production car on the road.

Cars and Bikes

motorcycles was not pursued with the same enthusiasm as cars. It was left to smaller companies and enthusiasts to build faster and faster bikes.

DeDion-Buton
In 1895, the French firm of DeDion-Buton built an engine that was to revolutionize the mass production of motorcycles. Small and light with a high-revving 138 cc four-stroke engine and advanced battery and coil ignition, this engine has been copied, used and developed by many famous motorcycle makers, including Harley-Davidson in the USA.

Early motorbike, 1913.

Fastest Bike
The Suzuki "Hayabusa" is the world's fastest production motorcycle and can easily exceed 186 mph (300 km/h). In fact, modern bike technology is so advanced that for road safety reasons major manufacturers have now agreed to limit the top speed of new road bikes to 186 mph (300 km/h).

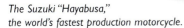

The Suzuki "Hayabusa," the world's fastest production motorcycle.

7

Planes

To most people, 200 years must seem like forever, but in terms of mechanical technology, it's really just a blink of an eye.

Planes

It's amazing that it has been barely 200 years since man first took flight in anything that resembled an airplane. Since the Wright brothers' first controlled flight, humans have flown to the moon and regularly travel at more than the speed of sound. Now that's technology!

Gliders

The father of the airplane was probably George Cayley. An Englishman, he first made a small model plane that actually flew in 1804, and five years later, in 1809, he made a full-size glider.

However, it was a further 40 years before he put together a triplane glider that carried the first passenger, in Brompton Dale, Yorkshire. Cayley's unnamed coachman was the world's first-known pilot!

Otto Lilienthal, a German aeronautics pioneer, made more than 2,000 flights in a glider that looked remarkably like a modern hang-glider. In 1895, he built a biplane incorporating a small motor to flap the wings, but a mechanical defect led to a fatal crash the following year.

Powered Plane

In 1874, Frenchman Felix Du Temple constructed the first powered plane to leave the ground, albeit in an uncontrolled flight. Amazingly, it was fitted with a retractable landing gear, too!

Otto Lilienthal.

Planes

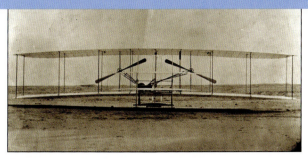

Flyer 1, made by the Wright brothers.

Controlled Flight

It was not until December 17th, 1903 that aviation could be considered a skill, because that was when the Wright brothers made the first controlled flight.

At Kittyhawk, North Carolina, Orville and Wilbur Wright took off, steered and landed an airplane. The plane was called *Flyer 1*. The Wright brothers' first plane was actually shorter than the wingspan of a modern jumbo jet, and was airborne for just twelve seconds.

First Accident

Orville Wright has another, less heroic, place in the aviation history books, because he was also responsible for the first known plane crash death! On September 7th, 1908, Orville took a Lieutenant Selfridge for a ride in his airplane. Unfortunately, the landing was not as controlled as Orville would have liked, and Selfridge was killed.

Warfare

Two world wars allowed for dramatic development of aircraft, as their usefulness in warfare was recognized. Almost all major aviation "firsts" were achieved in military aircraft or adaptations of them.

Non-Stop Flight

1919 saw the first direct non-stop transatlantic flight, in a World War One Vickers Vimy bomber, by British pilots John Alcock and Arthur Brown.

Jet Aircraft

The first known jet aircraft to fly was a German Heinkel He-178 turbo jet, flown by Erich Warsitz in 1939. This aircraft later became infamous for its dramatic tendency to explode unexpectedly.

Planes

Aircraft travel faster than any other form of transport on Earth.

Bell X-1.

Supersonic
The first airplane to exceed the speed of sound (Mach 1), was the Bell X-1, piloted by Charles Yeager of the USAF in 1949. Aircraft now fly at speeds in excess of Mach 4, but have to be made of very advanced materials, as air friction would melt normal airplanes.

VTOL
The first successful demonstration of VTOL (Vertical Take Off & Landing) was by the Rolls-Royce '"Flying Bedstead," on August 3rd, 1954. The most famous development of this principle is the British Aerospace Harrier jump-jet.

Concorde
The world's first supersonic passenger service started in 1976 with the BAC/ Aerospatiale Concorde. This amazing aircraft stopped service in 2003 and offered the fastest transatlantic crossing available.

Rutan Voyager
At the other end of the speed and economy scale, lightweight aircraft were taken to extremes in 1986 when the first non-stop, unrefuelled,

Concorde.

Planes

A single-engined Cessna.

around-the-world flight was made. Dick Rutan and Jeana Yeager piloted the *Rutan Voyager* aircraft.

Learning to Fly
By the end of 2000, the Cessna Aircraft Company, based in Wichita, Kansas, had manufactured over 180,000 aircraft. One of the major reasons for the company's success is the popularity of models, such as the single-engine Cessna, in which people learn to fly.

Fastest Airplane
The fastest airplane in the world is the Lockheed SR-71A "Blackbird" spy plane. On July 28th, 1976 this awesome plane reached a speed of 2,193 mph (3,530 km/h).

That's about the same speed as a rifle bullet!

Lockheed SR-71A "Blackbird."

11

Boats

Rock drawings discovered on the banks of the Red Sea show that the Egyptians had boats around 4000 BC.

USS Nimitz.

Shape
The basic shape of boats hasn't changed much. They are still tub-shaped, pointed at one end and blunt at the other. However, advancing technology in building methods and materials has made it possible to build huge and/or fast ships.

The First Navy
The Egyptians created the first organized navy in 2300 BC. The Romans later built up a huge naval fleet of large ships rowed by hundreds of oarsmen. Naval battles were popular events in the Roman Games. The Emperor Claudius was famous for flooding entire river valleys and staging real "life and death" battles involving hundreds of ships and thousands of crewmen, usually slaves or paid mercenaries. These battles could last many days or weeks, and in one it was reported that more than 20,000 men were killed!

Size
For a long time, the size of ships was severely limited by the fact that wood was the only known construction material. However, from 1405 to around 1431, the Chinese developed the technology to build massive wooden ships. Some were 400 ft long and 160 ft wide. These ships were monsters when you consider that Christopher Columbus sailed to America in the 85 ft long *Santa Maria*.

Tankers
Tankers, ships designed to carry bulk liquid cargoes, especially petroleum, are the biggest ships afloat. In fact, they are the biggest moving

Boats

Tankers are huge cargo ships.

machines on earth. Tankers of 400,000–500,000 tons are quite common. These ships are more than 1,300 ft long, 185 ft wide and may need more than 18 miles to stop!

Warships

The biggest warships afloat are US Navy Aircraft carriers. Several ships, including the *USS Nimitz*, weigh in at 100,000 tons. *Nimitz* has almost four acres of deck and is 1,100 ft long. It can carry over 100 fighter aircraft. Modern warships, especially mine-sweepers, are often made of plastic. Materials technology means they are light and strong. Also, magnetic mines don't stick to them!

Luxury ship *The World*.

Luxury Ships

The world's most luxurious ship is probably the Norwegian-built *The World*. It has 110 fully furnished homes and a further 88 guest homes. Each home comes with a terrace, two or three bedrooms, a fully furnished kitchen, and large dining and living areas. The twelve-decked ship has a maximum speed of 18.5 knots.

Submarines

It seems strange that anybody would want to board a boat, and then sink it on purpose. But that is what submarine designers like to do.

A torpedo.

An early submarine.

Origins
The idea of a useable submarine goes back thousands of years. As long ago as 1578 William Bourne, an Englishman, drew plans for a submarine.

However, it wasn't until 1620 that a Dutchman, Cornelius van Drebbel, actually built a submarine that worked. His sub took its first trip in the River Thames, and managed to stay under water for three hours.

Military Use
Since the first submarines appeared, it has always been warfare that has driven their development forward. To this day, every submarine at sea is involved in military operations.

Turtle
The first military submarine was used during the American Revolution between 1776 and 1777. The *USS Turtle* was built by David Bushnell and was used against British warships. The *Turtle*, a wooden sub powered by hand-turned propellers, would sneak up to British ships and attach explosives to their hulls. It was fortunate

Submarines

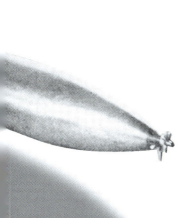

for the British that the explosives weren't much good and rarely went off.

Torpedoes
The development of submarines was slow until other factors improved—the only two things they are good at, staying underwater and firing torpedoes or missiles. The torpedo was designed in 1867 but it was too slow and unreliable to be an effective weapon. However, by the start of World War One torpedoes could reach speeds of 44 knots with a range of around 2.2 miles (3.5 km). Engines were usually diesel powered. Slow, noisy, and of limited range, they were the only choice until the early 1950s.

Nuclear Subs
The first nuclear submarine, the *Nautilus*, was launched in 1955. In 1958, *Nautilus* made the first voyage under the polar ice cap. The 1,830 mile (2,945 km) journey took six days. The first submerged nonstop circumnavigation of the world was made in 1960 by the nuclear submarine USS *Triton*. The first submarine built for the US Navy, the USS *Holland*, was completed on April 11th, 1900 and cost $150,000. Today's nuclear submarines cost more than $30,000,000, plus another $10,000,000 or more for the engine!

World's Smallest
The smallest submarine in the world was built in 1999. It is just 0.16 in. (4 mm) long and is so small that it was made using computer-guided lasers. This sub is not used in warfare, but instead travels around inside the human body to repair damage inside arteries and veins.

Captain Edward L. Beach looking through the periscope on the USS Triton.

Computers

Computers today are really the result of lots of different ideas, small inventions, and odd machines thought up, designed and built over the course of the last 2,000 years.

Difference Engine
Charles Babbage was the pioneer of mechanical computing. He thought he could eliminate errors in mathematical and astronomical tables by using machines that would both perform the calculations and print the results.

In 1822, he demonstrated a "difference engine," which could compile tables of logarithms, to the Royal Astronomical Society.

Unfortunately, the British government saw no future for computers and refused to pay for the development.

Stored-Program Computer
Konrad Zuse of Germany built the world's first working stored-program computer in 1941. His Z3 machine was based on electro-mechanical relays, and was used for military aircraft design.

Electronic Computers
Purely electronic computers were much faster than electro-mechanical ones. Among the earliest electronic computers were the Colossus computers, developed secretly in the UK from 1943. They unlocked coded German messages produced on sophisticated mechanical systems called Enigma machines.

Charles Babbage, pioneer of mechanical computing.

Computers

Modern-day shop cash registers depend on computers.

Everyday Use
Since these times, the development of computers has been fast and furious to the point that now it is impossible to avoid them. From cash registers and bar codes to car engines and space travel, virtually every aspect of modern life now depends on computers.

Without computers, many of the things in and around your home would be very different. Your parents will remember what TVs, cameras, and even washing machines were like before computers. Today, however, virtually every piece of electrical equipment made needs microchips and computerized circuits to work.

Microprocessors
Cramming an entire orchestra into a portable keyboard is only possible because of powerful microprocessors.

And what about compact discs, Nintendo® and Playstation®? Computers are making it possible to design and build everyday items more powerful and smaller than ever before.

Super Computers
Compared to the grinding cogs of the earliest mechanical computers, those of today can calculate at incredibly high speeds.

Computers that can execute instructions at speeds greater than 40 million instructions per second (MIPS) are quite common.

The ASCI White from IBM, a super computer.

17

Computers and the Internet

Computers can do so much, it is difficult to imagine a world without them.

The Internet
The Internet is a major development in distance communications. The precursor of the Internet was designed in America in 1969. Top military experts wanted a system of sending information across the telephone lines in a way that could not be interrupted. This was called ARPAnet.

College students discovered "the Net," and hacked into it to send messages and information to students at other universities. Soon businesses wanted to use the Net and within just a few years the Internet covered the whole world.

World Wide Web
The real explosion of Internet use came about in 1990 when Tim Berners-Lee, an English computer scientist, invented the World Wide Web. Berners-Lee wrote the software to program the first-ever web browser. This allowed anyone with a computer and a telephone connection to use the Internet.

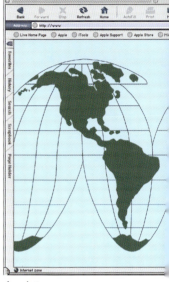

A web page.

Tim Berners-Lee invented the World Wide Web.

Computers and the Internet

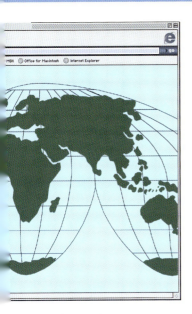

Growth
As a popular form of communication, the rapid growth of the Internet set a record. Radio took 38 years to reach 50 million users, television took thirteen years, and the personal computer a little over sixteen years. In comparison, the Internet got there in just four years after it was made available to the public!

Viruses
Viruses (programs that affect computer software) are the best-known and most troublesome problem associated with the Internet. Computer vandals (hackers) soon realized that viruses could be sent secretly to computers all over the world. Most viruses are quite harmless and are sent out as a joke but others cause huge amounts of damage.

Chernobyl
The world's most damaging virus was written by a student. Called the Chernobyl virus, it was started on the twelfth anniversary of the Chernobyl nuclear explosion. Since April 26th, 1998 it has affected over one million computers.

The Chernobyl virus damages the machine's operating system and makes it useless.

Friendly Viruses
The friendliest viruses are written by programmers working for major companies. These programs are hidden in common software applications and are completely harmless yet fun. Called "Easter eggs," they are found by using a secret set of mouse clicks or keystrokes when using the software.

I Love You
The most widespread virus in the world even forced the closure of the White House for a time. The "I Love You" virus was started on May 1st, 2000. It spread through e-mail and within just four days had mutated into three different generations. By May 8th, 2002, "I Love You" had infected no less than 3.1 million computers across the world.

Computers and the Home

Computers are inside many things found in the home.

The PS2.

Computer Games
Computer games have probably made more of modern technology than any other day-to-day item. The world's first computer games were "Mario Brothers" and "Donkey Kong," which have sold more than one million units each since they were launched.

Unfortunately Internet technology, recordable CDs, and powerful PCs have meant that millions of games are believed to have been illegally copied.

Best Sellers
The best-selling games console is easily the Sony Playstation®. Including the PS2, it has sold more than 80 million units since it was launched.

Multiple Play
The Internet added a new and unlimited dimension to computer gaming with multiple play games. People can log on to games sites and compete with multiple players via the Internet.

Domestic Appliances
In a modern home, just about any electrical item that has a program or an operating cycle will have a microprocessor chip to control it. When you go to bed, check out the clock/radio alarm if you have one. All those functions tucked into that little box are only possible with microprocessors.

Computers and the Home

Before the arrival of the microchip, the washing machine and dishwasher had very basic controls. On or off was as much as some could manage. Now computers can program these machines to carry out complicated jobs hours or days in advance.

Microwaves

Microwave cookers for the catering trade were first sold in the USA around 1953, but domestic microwaves did not achieve widespread popularity until about 1980. When microwave cookers were first introduced, many people believed that food cooked in them could be radioactive. Microwaves work by making the watery molecules in the food move so rapidly that they heat up and cook it from the inside out.

Television

John Logie Baird demonstrated the first moving picture show on a television in 1927. In less than 80 years, and thanks to computers, we have satellite TV in glorious color, cable TV with multiple channels and sets that can store hundreds of movies and TV programs.

A plasma screen television.

The latest televisions have "plasma" or flat screens. They have excellent clarity and color and minimal problems with reflection.

MP3

The MP3 enables people to download music direct from the Internet. The world's smallest MP3 player is the size of a wrist watch, but still has 64 MB of memory.

Robots

Robots are extremely powerful or well-programmed computers that can "remember" and later act upon input from sensors or the programmer. Androids (human-like robots) may look smart, but true intelligence is really not possible.

The Dyson DC06 robotic vacuum cleaner.

Industrial Robots

Industrial robots look nothing like humans. The fact is that robots only have to work. To make them look like a person is just a bit of very expensive fun.

Home Help

If you want a little help with your chores, the Dyson company makes the world's most advanced robotic vacuum cleaner. It is loaded with lots of sensors and computer chips.

The technology hidden inside the DC06 enables it to "learn" the layout of rooms and the position of furniture. Once the DC06 has got its bearings, it can vacuum a house without any human input, apart from switching it on and off.

Tamogotchi

CyberPets are one of the most popular home robots. It all started with that little monster in a box, the Tamogotchi. This apparent cyber life-form was all the rage a few years ago and came in every shape imaginable. Tamogotchis sold in millions and at one time were the fastest-selling toy in the world. Interestingly, around 80% of owners were girls.

A Tamogotchi.

Robots

Cyberpets
CyberPets tagged along behind the Tamogotchi. But now puppies and cats, even spiders and scorpions, can be at your command. Robot pets are all just remote-controlled toys that are programmed to respond to a few basic actions.

Industrial Robots
Robotics is the science and technology of machines designed to function in place of human beings, in order to carry out tasks automatically. The name "robot" was first used in 1920 in a play about a man who builds a robot which later kills him.

A precision robot spot welding a suspension unit.

"Robot" comes from a Czech word, "robota," which means "drudgery." The first practical robotics were designed by the British inventor C. W. Kenward in 1957. These robots later became the first used for industrial automation.

Precision Robots
A robot which could properly handle a tool (for painting) was first used in Norway in 1966. Since then, there has been a continual evolution towards robots of greater precision, such as the Japanese selective compliance assembly robot arm (SCARA).

A robot pet.

Robots

Modern Robots
A modern robot has a mechanical manipulator (usually an arm) and sensors controlled by a computer. Early hydraulically-powered robots have given way to direct-drive machines using electric motors. The main goal of robot research in artificial intelligence is to enable robots to sense and move intelligently around their environment.

The PUMA
The most widely used industrial robot is the PUMA, designed in Switzerland in the 1970s. This robot is most common in laboratories and automated assembly lines. More cars are now made by robots than by humans.

Minerva
In July 1999, a humanoid robot called *Minerva* enjoyed a two-week

long stint as a tour guide around the Smithsonian National Museum of American History. She acted on the information sent to her computer via her multiple sensors, which made her capable of showing guests around the exhibits. She'd also blast her horn loudly when objects blocked her path!

Remote Control
Ever since bombs were first used, people have been hurt trying to defuse ones that have failed to explode at the right time. However, in

A car factory production line.

Robots

Minerva robot. Image courtesy of the Lemelson Center for the Study of Invention and Innovation. Charles Townes, photographer, Smithsonian Institution.

1972, the British Army introduced a remote-controlled robot to defuse bombs. It includes a battery-operated motor and a selection of mechanical arms. A television camera sends a picture to the operator's monitor. Various devices help the robot get in and out of doors and windows, and it carries a kind of water cannon for flushing out explosives. Newer versions of these robots can also fire a gun into bombs to explode them. This often destroys the robot, but at least no humans get injured.

Android
The most humanoid robot (android) ever built was called simply *P3*. Built in 1977, *P3* is just 4.2 ft high, with two arms and two legs.

It took 150 engineers eleven years to produce at a cost of $75,000,000. Even though *P3* appears to be very intelligent, it can only do what it is programmed to do.

P3 — the most humanoid robot ever built.

Satellites in Space

Any chunk of rock orbiting a planet is a satellite, even if the rock is huge. Earth is a satellite of the Sun. Artificial satellites are usually unmanned spacecraft orbiting Earth or another planet.

Origins

Although the first artificial satellite, *Sputnik 1*, was launched on October 4th, 1957, the idea of an artificial satellite goes back to Isaac Newton. He showed that if an object was projected above the Earth's atmosphere with a speed in excess of 5 miles per second (8 km/s) in a direction roughly parallel to the Earth's surface it would go into an elliptical (oval) orbit around the Earth.

Explorer 1.

The First Satellite

The USA's first satellite, *Explorer 1*, flew in February 1958; it carried instruments that revealed the presence of radiation belts around Earth.

Skylab.

Satellites in Space

Mir
Up to March 2000, the largest man-made object in space was the Russian *Mir* space station. *Mir* weighed more than 286,500 lb (130 tonnes), and orbited Earth for almost fifteen years. When *Mir* was scrapped, it was deliberately made to re-enter Earth's atmosphere. Chunks of red-hot *Mir* produced an amazing shower of fire when they re-entered. *Mir* was also involved in the first-ever space crash when it collided with an unmanned cargo ship.

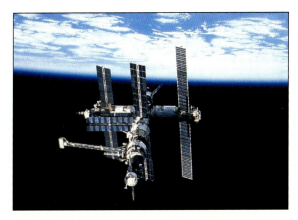

Since then, over 5,000 satellites have been launched, several hundred of which are currently operational. They include meteorological satellites, scientific satellites, Earth resources satellites, military satellites, communications satellites, and navigation satellites.

Space Stations
As the rockets to launch satellites have become more powerful, ever larger objects can be sent into space. Space stations are usually sent up in bits and assembled by astronauts in space. The largest single satellite ever launched was America's *SkyLab* in 1973. This piece of kit was no less than 82 ft long and weighed in at over 59,000 lb (26,762 kg).

Communications Satellites
Communications satellites are used for worldwide telephone, television, and data communication. Satellites work by using microwaves which are able to carry vast amounts of information. The microwaves are, however, easily absorbed by solid objects, so both transmitter and receiver need to be in line of sight. Satellites provide a method of achieving line-of-sight communication over long distances.

Telecommunication

Satellites enable us to make phone calls to virtually every location in the world.

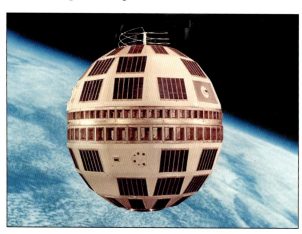

The Telstar *satellite.*

First Telephone
Alexander Graham Bell patented the first telephone receiver and transmitter in the UK and the USA during 1876. Bell was so excited, he boasted that he could imagine the day when every town in America would have its own phone! Now, tens of millions of people around the world have telephones. Instead of the messages running along copper wire to the next town, they are bounced into space and then rebounded around the world.

Telstar
In 1962, the Bell Telephone Company launched *Telstar*, an active satellite with its own solar power source to boost the signals, which enabled the first live television broadcast from the USA to Europe to be made.

Geostationary Satellites
By 1963, rockets sufficiently powerful to place a satellite in geostationary orbit were available. *Syncom 1*, a US satellite for telephone and telex use, was the first geostationary satellite.

The first commercial geostationary satellite was *Early Bird* or *Intelsat 1*, launched in 1965. *Intelsat* soon had three satellites over the Atlantic, Pacific, and Indian oceans for worldwide coverage.

Today
Today, numerous communications satellites orbit the Earth. Modern communications satellites can handle tens of thousands of telephone calls, plus radio and television broadcasts simultaneously.

Telecommunication

Downsizing
After Alexander Graham Bell launched his telephone machine and Intelsat launched their communication satellites, the world became very small. People could speak to each other across the world as if they were next door. The next big breakthrough in communications was cellphones, the smaller and more powerful the better.

Cellphones
The first cellular telephone was demonstrated in Chicago during 1977, and introduced to the UK in 1985. These phones had big, heavy batteries, about the size of a shoe box, and a handset about the size of a regular telephone.

Cellphones are called cell phones because the system involves dividing the country into areas or "cells" about 1–8 miles (2–13 km) in radius. A cellphone caller connects with the nearest transmitter in his cell. The mobile units must be able to re-tune to a new frequency as they pass from one cell to another, a process that needs a very advanced electronic switching system served by satellites.

Satellite Phones
Satellite telephones that can be used with a direct Earth-to-satellite link are used by explorers and expedition members who are in remote areas where no network cells exist. These are briefcase size, are very expensive to buy and have the most expensive call charges in the world.

Mini Mobiles
These days mobile phones are so tiny you can fit them in your pocket. The Ericsson T66 is just 3.6 in. x 1.6 in x 0.7 in. and weighs a featherweight 2.1 ounces.

Technology and the Environment

Advanced technology is not all about going further, faster and doing more damage when we get there. Across the world environmental protection is an important issue and obtaining power from renewable and non-polluting sources is a huge challenge.

Wind Power

The wind offers possibly the best opportunity for power generation as it is freely available. In many countries giant wind generators are already producing pollution-free power.

In California, wind farms with dozens of generators are already supplying more than 1% of the state's electricity needs. In Denmark it is twice this amount.

In the UK the first giant wind generator was built in Norfolk. This machine is mounted on a tower over 300 ft tall and can produce enough electricity to power 10,000 local homes.

Hydrogen Cars

Car manufacturers are also in a race to produce a truly pollution-free car.

Wind turbines producing electricity.

Technology and the Environment

The Tulip, an electric-powered concept car.

Electricity has been the front runner for several years but hydrogen is now the long-term favorite because the only by-product of burning hydrogen, to create power, is water.

Clockwork

Any advance in technology which doesn't require the use of non-renewable fuels is welcome. One benefit of modern technology is that it has often made it possible for inventors to take old ideas and bring them up to date. Very often people think these inventions are new but it's only the materials or functions that are new. For many years machines that today run on batteries, mains electricity or solar power were wound up.

Clockwork did just what it says, it made clocks work. Many other things were also clockwork but old springs and cogs were not very efficient so limited its use.

Modern materials and lighter, but stronger, components have made it possible to reinvent clockwork. Trevor Bayliss, an English inventor, developed a modern version of a wind-up radio that far

Trevor Bayliss.

exceeds the performance of any others. This radio has brought news, information and music to millions of people in remote or undeveloped countries.

A clockwork radio.

31

Gadgets and Gizmos

Gadgets and Gizmos

A good gadget should be far more ingenious than it is useful. That's why millions of gadgets are bought every year by people who don't need them. They just want them!

Gadgets

People tend to think that modern technology means computers or electronics but gadgets write their own rules. Materials technology has allowed great advancement in the design field. All sorts of things can be dreamed up or made ever smaller as a result of new technology. But some of the best-selling gadgets are some of the oldest.

Smallest Computer

In the battle to be smallest even the thinnest laptop computers have been beaten by a fully functional hand-held PC. The Tiqit is a powerful Pentium computer that is little bigger than a hand-held game console. With a full keyboard, full color screen and plenty of memory the Tiqit is a serious piece of kit.

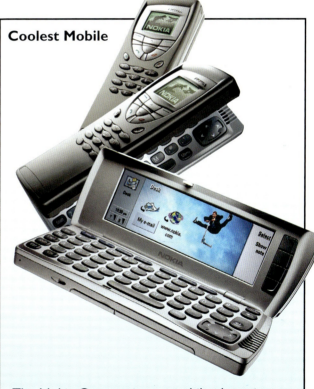

Coolest Mobile

The Nokia Communicator mobile phone is great for texting, as it has a full keyboard. You can write and send faxes, access the Internet and it's also a powerful computer.

Tiqit (pictured left).

Gadgets and Gizmos

Smallest Server
The smallest Internet web server computer in the world is only about the size of a normal-sized match head! This minute piece of technology runs an entire website base in America.

Swiss Army Knife
Engineering technology made it possible to make small metal items with great accuracy and so the famous Swiss Army knife got more and more blades and tools. Knives with up to 20 tools are quite common but the world record stands at 300! To list all of the tools would be too boring but they were there and they all worked. It was pretty heavy though.

A Swiss Army knife.

Remote Control
Almost every home in the world has one or maybe several of the world's best-selling gadget.

A remote control.

The remote control, the 'zapper', started life as just a TV controller. Now they control distant entertainment systems or garage doors. They will open and close curtains and even run the bath. The first TV remote was designed in 1950 in America. The device was called "LazyBones" and quickly became a must-have gadget.

GPS Watch
This is an example of a not particularly useful gadget. Apart from telling the time, this watch will tell you exactly where you are in the world.

Gadgets and Gizmos

Portable Phone Charger
Nokia have introduced a very handy gadget to have, a portable mobile phone charger you can attach to your keyring. Really just a battery that you connect to your phone, it will provide about an hour of power.

Digital Camera
One of the most popular digital cameras is l'espion. About the size of a matchbox, it is capable of storing up to 80 pictures.

A l'espion digital camera.

Transformer Toys
Gadget toys have appeared in their hundreds as follow-ons from TV and movie heroes. The Transformer range of toys that can be twisted, clicked and turned into a variety of objects has sold millions of units across the world.

A Transformer toy.

Lethal Weapons

People are continually looking for ways to make weapons more effective and efficient.

Fighter Aircraft
On October 5th, 1914, just after the start of World War One, a French "Voisin" airplane was the first ever to shoot down another plane. The passenger used a machine gun to shoot down a German "Aviatik". Both sides immediately saw the potential of airplanes as lethal weapons.

Development
Through two wars the development of war planes was furious. By the end of World War Two planes were firing multiple machine guns, dropping massive bombs and firing deadly torpedoes at ships around the world.

Today
The latest fighter aircraft travel at twice the speed of sound and are equipped with missiles that are guided very accurately. Another recent development is the US F-117 "Stealth" Fighter, designed to be invisible to radar.

Fighter Ships
Advances in military ships and submarines have run more or less simultaneously since World War One. Surface ships at first got much bigger so that huge numbers of heavy guns could be carried.

Modern Missiles
Modern naval warfare is dependent on the newest computer-guided missiles which are smaller, lighter and

F-117 "Stealth" Fighters.

Lethal Weapons

The "Voisin" airplane.

far more powerful than older guns and shells. Modern, high-tech warships are themselves much smaller, lighter and more advanced than any before.

Modern missile weapons are deadly over a range of hundreds of miles.

Military Submarines

The first military submarines like USS Turtle could submerge for only a matter of hours and were armed only with unreliable mines.

The nuclear-powered subs developed since the first one, the USS Nautilus, can remain fully submerged and silent for weeks or months if needed. Submarines are also the main carriers of nuclear weapons and missiles that can be launched from below the surface for many hundreds of miles.

The USS Nautilus.

Lethal Weapons

A fighter-bomber.

Torpedoes

In 1867, Robert Whitehead, a British engineer, developed the locomotive torpedo, which carried an explosive warhead and was powered by compressed air.

By the start of World War One torpedoes propelled by an engine burning an air, water vapor and oil mixture could reach speeds of 44 knots. The first known sinking of a ship using an air-launched torpedo was in August 1915. During World War Two torpedoes sank huge numbers of warships and cargo ships. Today's torpedoes all possess high-tech homing mechanisms or are remotely guided.

Dropping Bombs

Bombs were first dropped from aircraft during World War One but were no more than bundles of explosives. The fuse was lit in the plane and the bomb then released as quickly as possible.

The aftereffects of a nuclear strike.

Lethal Weapons

Nuclear Bombs
The most powerful bombs in the world are nuclear bombs. One of these bombs was exploded over the Japanese city of Hiroshima on August 6th, 1945. Almost the entire city was obliterated.

Chemical Weapons
The use of poisonous substances such as disease germs to kill or injure the enemy has been developed since World War One when mustard gas was used. Other substances include chlorine, and phosgene. Nerve gases, chemicals that strip the leaves from entire forests, viruses and bacteria (for example, anthrax) are also used.

Protection
Modern chemical weapons are very advanced and may be delivered by long-range artillery, missile, or sprayed from aircraft. The main defense against them is protective clothing, gas masks and special suits made of rubber or treated cloth.

Chemical and biological warfare response team.

Rockets

All rockets basically consist of a long tube filled with some sort of fuel that, when ignited, will fire the tube into the air. Rockets have been used as fireworks for thousands of years and have been developed to launch satellites, warheads and space missions.

Missile or Rocket?
What is the difference between a rocket and a missile? Not much. A missile is any object thrown through the air. A rocket is really just a self-propelled missile. In modern terms a rocket that delivers an explosion is usually called a missile. Ones that launch other, less dangerous, objects or people into space are called rockets. But NASA likes to call them rocket-powered launch vehicles. Simple isn't it?

Early Experiments
The Chinese have been making and using rocket fireworks since around 1300 BC, when gunpowder was used to boost the flight of arrows. It was also the Chinese who first attempted to send a person into space. The ancient Chinese once fixed lots of small rockets to a wooden chair, sat their emperor on it and attempted to assist him in reaching the heavens. Unfortunately both the chair and the emperor disappeared in a cloud of smoke!

Gunpowder Rocket
During the Middle Ages, the gunpowder rocket was adapted for military use in the form of flaming arrows. These were fired from a bow like mini missiles. They were not very effective

Rockets

A V2 rocket.

The first truly guided missiles were used operationally during World War Two, when Germany bombarded London and other cities with the V2 rocket, a ballistic missile, and the V1 pulse jet, a primitive cruise missile.

Blue Flame

Even car and motorcycle builders attempting to break world speed records have discovered the benefits of rocket power.

A rocket-propelled car, *Blue Flame,* set a land speed record traveling at more than 700 mph!

against people but very good at setting fire to straw roofs and frightening horses.

The war rocket was further developed in the early nineteenth century by William Congreve in the UK. These rockets, which were unguided and inaccurate, were mass-bombardment weapons. Similar but much modernized versions of these solid-fuel powered rockets are still widely used today.

Guided Missiles

Guided missiles were possible only after the development of radio and electronics. Early prototypes, which were, in fact, pilotless radio-controlled model aircraft, appeared in the 1920s and 1930s.

The rocket-propelled Blue Flame.

41

Space Exploration

Some truly amazing feats have occurred with space exploration missions.

The world's largest optical and infrared telescope – the Keck Telescope.

The Keck Telescope

Keeping an eye on a satellite or an exploration craft as it journeys to other galaxies requires a telescope that is out of this world. The twin Keck Telescope is the world's largest optical and infrared telescope. Built on the island of Hawaii, each tower is eight storeys high and weighs 3,300 ton. Fitted with an enormous 32 ft mirror, the Keck can see a golf ball 93 miles (150 km) away.

Manned Space Travel

In 1957 Russia launched the *Sputnik I* satellite into orbit around the earth and a little dog called Laika became the first space traveler. Since then many billions of dollars and rubles have been spent sending people and machines into space.

Space Shuttle

Since these early flights, many hundreds of satellites have been launched and many hundreds of rockets have become "space scrap". However, the cost and the loss of technology every time a rocket was used led scientists to develop a reusable space craft. The Space Shuttle, which began flights in 1981, was the result. The Shuttle has a

Space Exploration

main vehicle with three rocket motors (the orbiter), two solid-fuelled rocket boosters that are dumped two minutes after takeoff and later recovered, and a non-recoverable external fuel tank. The orbiter can carry a cargo of up to about 33 tons. On re-entry, the orbiter is flown like a glider, and lands on a runway. Space shuttles have been used over and over again and have carried many hundreds of tons of equipment into space.

The Space Shuttle.

The First Man in Space

Yuri Gagarin became the world's first astronaut in 1961. Gagarin was aboard the Russian *Vostok 1* satellite. He made just one orbit of the earth before returning safely to a hero's welcome. One year later John Glenn was the first American to orbit the earth. He was launched in the *Mercury-Atlas 6* and completed three orbits.

Yuri Gagarin.

Spectacular Failures

Since the ancient Chinese blew up a chair along with their emperor, many rockets have failed. Ancient rockets could only be tested by letting them off and hoping for the best.

A failed V1 rocket.

Danger
Unfortunately the 'best' was often a big bang at the wrong time! Setting light to a big tube packed with explosives has always been quite a dangerous thing to do. Put wings onto the rocket, sit people inside and set light to it and it soon becomes very dangerous.

Modern technology means that rocket scientists can use huge computers like the IBM RS/2000 to simulate rocket flights. They can even pretend to crash them. Now that's a computer game!

V1 Rockets
The German V1 rockets used to bomb London during World War Two were notorious for exploding on takeoff. Luckily the people involved could hide in shelters and, as the rockets were unmanned, there was little loss of life.

Heinkel He-178
The first jet aircraft to fly was the German Heinkel He-178. It was hoped that this remarkable plane would help to destroy the British Air Force. Unfortunately for the

Spectacular Failures

early pilots the Heinkel killed many more of them than the intended English airmen.

A successful takeoff was rare as the Heinkel had a habit of exploding before it left the ramp. Of those that did become airborne, flights were often short before the plane exploded. It is thought that as many as 60% of He-178 flights ended in a ball of flames.

Alan Shepard.

Worst Launch
The worst space launch failure ever was when the US Space Shuttle *Challenger* exploded shortly after takeoff. A fuel tank had split during the takeoff and the leaking fuel turned *Challenger* into a bomb. Seven astronauts were killed in a massive fireball.

Shortest Space Flight
The shortest space flight ever was by an American, Alan Shepard. Shephard had traveled just 187.49 km (116 miles) into space before it became obvious that his rocket wasn't powerful enough to get him into orbit. So poor Shepard had to come straight back down. The flight lasted just 15 minutes 28 seconds.

Glossary

Confused by any terms used in this book? Check their meanings here.

Airplane generally means a heavier-than-air aircraft.

Androids robots with the appearance of humans.

ARPAnet the precursor of the Internet.

Astronaut a person trained for traveling in space.

Beetle Volkswagen motor car. The world's best-selling car.

Bell X-1 the first airplane to exceed the speed of sound (Mach 1).

Bit in computer technology, a single binary digit represented either by "0" or "1". The smallest unit of information.

Blackbird the Lockheed SR-71A spy plane. The world's fastest airplane.

Blue Flame a rocket-propelled car which set a land speed record of 700 mph.

Bugatti Italian motor car manufacturer. Built the Veyron supercar.

Bytes in computer technology, a group of bits, usually eight or six, processed as a single unit of data.

Chemical warfare the use of chemical or biological weapons in war or terrorism.

Chernobyl the Chernobyl virus was the world's most damaging computer virus.

Colossus early electronic computers developed to break German wartime secret codes.

Concorde the world's first supersonic passenger airplane.

Easter eggs fun programs hidden within other software packages.

Fly-by-wire the process of controlling aircraft with computers rather than mechanically connected controls.

Gadget a small mechanical device or appliance. Usually designed for its novelty value rather than its practicality.

Gunpowder an explosive mixture of potassium nitrate, charcoal and sulphur.

Hacker someone who is interested in obtaining unauthorized access to computer programs or systems.

Harley-Davidson famous American motorcycle manufacturers.

Horsepower a unit of power, originally based on the estimated pulling power of a horse.

I love you the world's most widespread computer virus. Started in May 2000.

Internet the worldwide network of linked computers.

Jet a thrust motor that uses heat to super-expand air that is "squirted" out of the engine in order to produce thrust.

Lazybones the world's first TV remote controller.

Glossary

Mach 1 the speed of sound.

Microwave electromagnetic radiation waves used in cooking or radar.

Minesweeper naval ship used to locate and destroy marine mines.

Motorcycle a two-wheeled powered vehicle.

NASA the American National Aeronautics and Space Administration.

Pentium a computer-processing chip and a trademark of the Intel Corporation of America.

Prototype the first object or machine made of a new design.

Punchcards paper cards with punched holes. The first method of passing instructions and data to electro-mechanical computers.

RAM a computer's Random Access Memory.

Robot a machine programmed to carry out mechanical function in the manner of a person.

Satellite any natural or artificial object orbiting a planet.

Shuttle Reusable space craft.

Solar power power generated or sourced from the heat of the sun.

Sound barrier a pressure barrier met by vehicles about to exceed the speed of sound.

Sputnik 1 the first satellite to orbit the earth with a live passenger—a dog called Laika.

Stealth Fighter American military aircraft, designed to be almost invisible to radar.

Submarine any craft that can operate below the water's surface.

Super computer a general term used to describe computers that can execute instructions at speeds greater than 40 million instructions per second (MIPS).

Supersonic a speed faster than the speed of sound.

Tin Lizzie nickname of Henry Ford's first mass-produced motor car.

Torpedo self-propelled, explode on contact, submarine missile.

Virus a slang term for a program written and introduced to computer systems without the permission of the owner.

VTOL Vertical Take Off & Landing.

Web server a computer dedicated to processing applications and access to the Internet.

World Wide Web a channel of the Internet accessed and used via computers with "browser" software which reads and translates a unique text-writing language.

Z3 the world's first working stored-program computer, built in 1941 by Konrad Zuse.

Finding Out More

Got the techno-bug?

As technology advances at a spectacular rate, keeping up to date with the latest ideas is vital. To discover more about today's technology check out some of these sources.

Library
Get to know your local library. The whole world's knowledge is right there in books.

Bookshops
See what bookshops have to offer. Most bookshops will stock copies of *The Guinness Book of Records* or *Encyclopaedia Britannica*.

Magazines
There are many magazines available from newsagents with lots of info on the latest technological advances.

Internet
Ask an adult to help you search the internet. There are lots of websites with info and fun stuff for kids relating to the latest gadgets and advances in technology.